A.K BIOLOGY CLASS 9TH

NOTES + IMPORTANT QUESTION + MCQ + NCERT SOLUTION + SAMPLE PAPER

DR. ABHISHEK KUMAR

This book is dedicated to every teacher who loves to

teache but hates all the crap that comes with it ....

DR. ABHISHEK KUMAR

Contents

I

THE FUNDAMENTAL UNIT OF LIFE

Facts that Matter

The smallest functional unit of life is a cell, discovered by Robert Hooke in 1665. A cell can independently perform all necessary activities to sustain life. Hence cell is the basic unit of life.
There are two types of cells **plant cell** and **animal cell.** The different cell organelles and their functions are as follows:

Cellular respiration

Cellular respiration is the process by which the food releases energy in the mitochondria. Cells absorb glucose from the food and burn it to produce energy.

1. Plasma/Cell membrane: This is the outermost covering of the cell that separates the contents of the cell from its external environment. The plasma membrane allows or permits the entry and exit of some materials in and out of the cell so the cell membrane is called a selectively permeable membrane.

Some substances like CO2 or O2 gases can move across the cell membrane by a process called **diffusion.**

The movement of water molecules (liquid) through such a selectively permeable membrane is called **osmosis.** Osmosis is the passage of water from a region of high water concentration through a semi-permeable membrane to a region of low water concentration.

If the medium surrounding the cell has a higher water concentration than the cell, the cell will gain water by osmosis. Such a solution is known as a **hypotonic solution.**

If the medium has exactly the same water concentration as the cell, there will be no net movement of water across the cell membrane. Such a solution is known as an **isotonic solution**.

If the medium has a lower water concentration then the cell will lose water by osmosis. Such a solution is known as a **hypertonic solution**

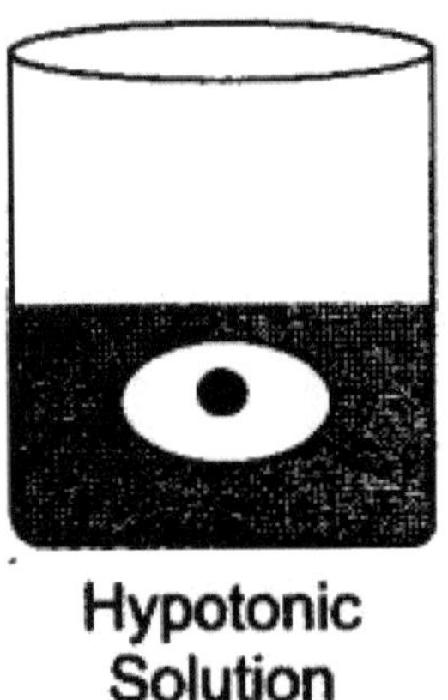

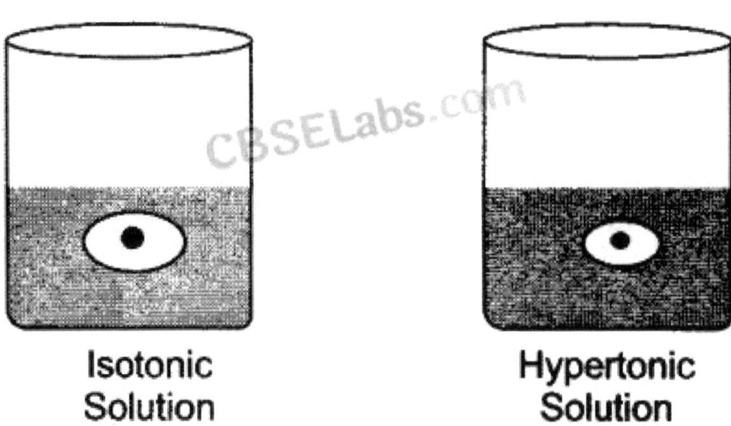

The plasma membrane is flexible and is made up of organic molecules called lipids and proteins. The flexibility of cell membrane also enables the cell to engulf in food and other material from its external environment. Such process is known as **endocytosis**. It is observed in Amoeba.

Cell wall (Protective wall):

Plants cells, in addition to the plasma membrane have another rigid outer covering called **cell wall.**

The cell wall lies outside the **plasma membrane.**

The plant cell wall is mainly composed of cellulose.

It is a complex substance and provides structural strength to plant cells.

When a living plant loses water through osmosis there is shrinkage or contraction of contents of the cell away from cell wall. This phenomenon is known as **plasmolysis.**

Nucleus (Brain of a cell):

The nucleus has a double-layered covering called nuclear membrane. The nuclear membrane has pores which allow the transfer of material from inside the nucleus to its outside, i.e., to the cytoplasm.

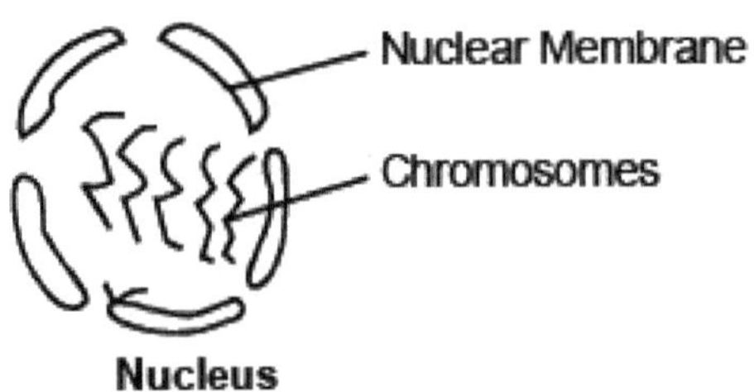

Nucleus

The nucleus contains chromosomes, which are visible as rod-shaped structures only when the cell is about to divide.

Chromosomes

Chromosomes contain information for inheritance of features from parents to next generation in form of DNA [Deoxyribo Nucleic Acid] molecules.

Chromosomes are composed of DNA and protein.
Functional segments of DNA are called **genes.**
The nucleus plays a central role in cellular reproduction.

Prokaryotic Cells:

In some organisms like bacteria, the nuclear material is not enclosed by nuclear membrane and membrane bound cell organelle are absent. Such nucleus is called **nucleoid** and such cells are known as **prokaryoticcell**. Such cells have single chromosome.

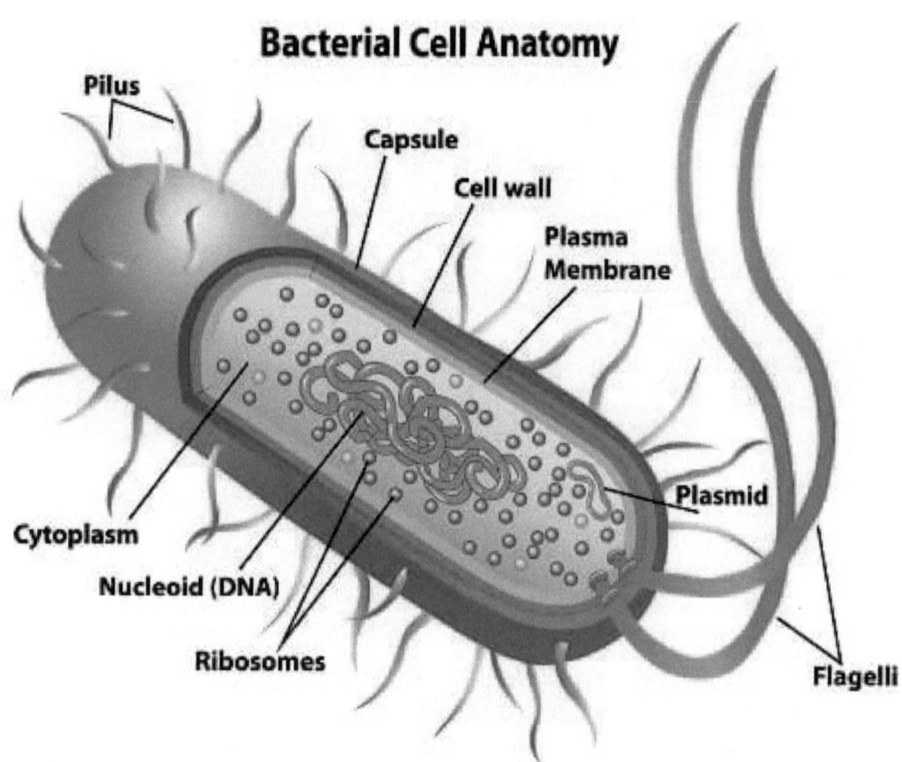

Eukaryotic Cells:

Cells having well defined nucleus and having membrane bound cell organelle is termed as eukaryotic cell. Such cells have more than one chromosomes.

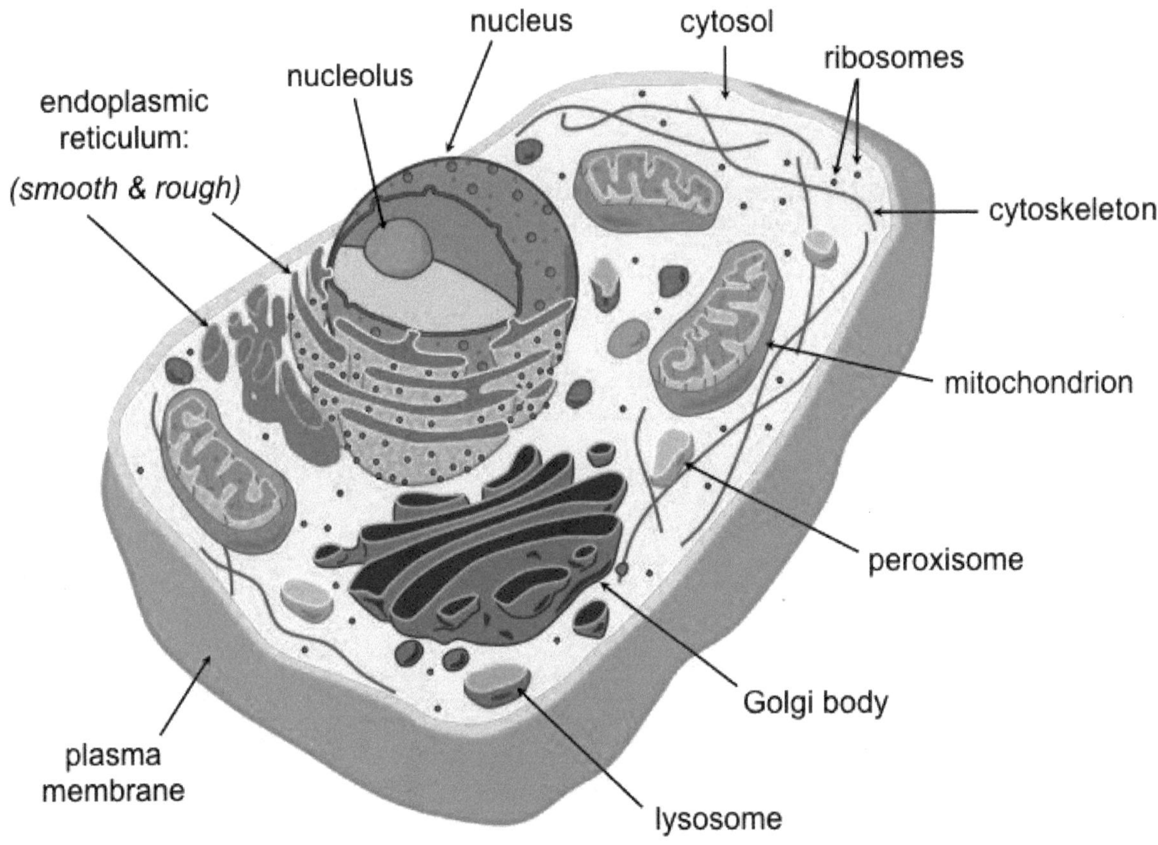

Cytoplasm:

The cytoplasm is the fluid content inside the plasma membrane. It also contains many specialised cell organelles. Each of these organelles performs a specific function for the cell.

Cell Organelles:

Every cell has a membrane around it to keep its content separate from the external environment. The different components of cell perform different function and these components are called cell organelles.

Endoplasmic Reticulum (ER) (Channels, Network for transport):

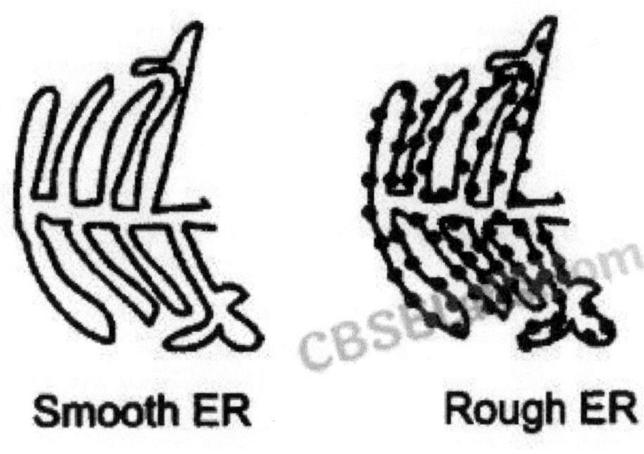

The ER is a large network of membrane-bound tubes and sheets. It looks like long tubules or round or oblong bags. There are two types of ER-**Rough endoplasmic reticulum [RER]** and **smooth endoplasmic reticulum [SER].**

RER has particles called **ribosomes** attached to its surface. The ribosomes Endoplasmic Reticulum are the sites of protein manufacture.

The SER helps in the manufacture of fat molecules, or lipids, important for cell function. Some of these proteins and lipids help in building the cell membrane. This process is known as **membrane biogenesis.** Some other proteins and lipids function as enzymes and hormones.

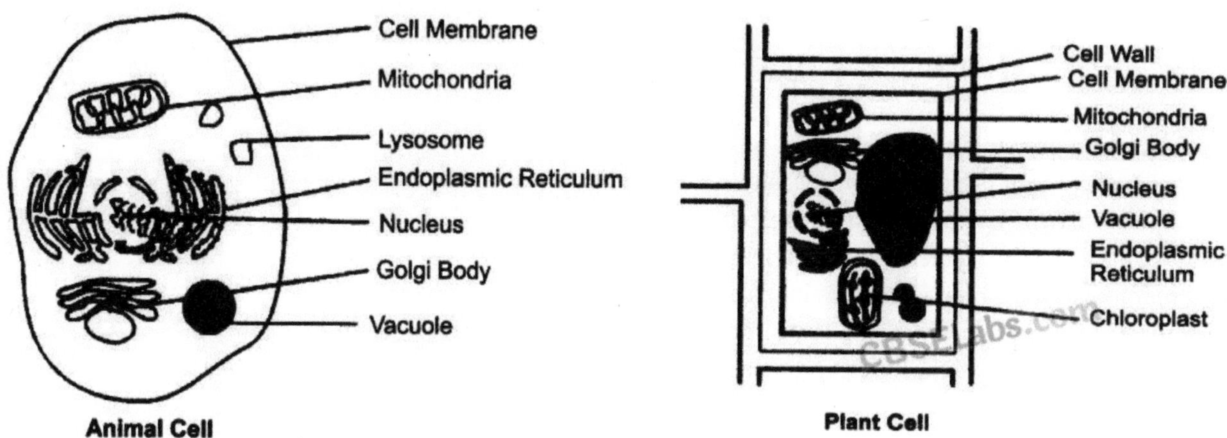

The one function of ER is to serve as channels for the transport of materials between various regions of the cytoplasm or between the cytoplasm and the nucleus. The ER also functions as a cytoplasmic framework providing a surface for some of the biochemical activities of the cell.

Golgi Apparatus (Packaging):

The golgi apparatus, first described by Camillo Golgi, consists of a system of membrane-bound vesicles arranged approximately, parallel to each other in stacks called **cisterns.**

The material synthesised near the ER is packaged and dispatched to various targets inside and outside the cell through the Golgi apparatus. It's function include the storage, modification and packages of products in vesicles. In some cases complex sugar may be made from simple sugar in the Golgi apparatus. It is also involved in the formation of lysosomes.

Lysosomes [Suichge bags] (Cleanliness of cell):

Lysosomes are a kind of waste dispatch and disposal system of the cell.

Lysosome help to keep the cell clean by digesting any foreign material as well as worn-out cell organelles.

Foreign materials entering the cells such as bacteria or food, as well as old organelles, end up in the lysosome, which break them up into small pieces.

They are able to do this because they contain powerful digestive enzymes capable of breaking down all organic material. Under abnormal condition, when the cell gets damaged, lysosomes may burst and the enzymes digest their own cell. Therefore they are also known as "suicide bags"

Mitochondria (Powerhouse, Energy provider):

Mitochondria are known as powerhouses of the cell.

The energy required for various chemical activities needed for life is released by mitochondria in the form of ATP [Adenosine Triphosphate] molecules.

ATP is known as energy currency of the cell.

Mitochondria have two membrane coverings instead of just one.

The outer membrane is very porous while the inner membrane is deeply folded.

They are able to make some of their own protein.

Plastids:

Plastids are present only in plant cells.

There are two types of plastids chromoplasts and leucoplasts.

Chromoplasts are the coloured plastids present in leaves, flowers and fruits.

Plastids containing the pigment chlorophyll are known as **chloroplasts.**

They are important for photosynthesis in plants.

Chloroplasts also contain various yellow or orange pigments in addition to chlorophyll.

Leucoplasts are found primarily in organelles in which materials such as starch, oils and protein granules are stored.

The internal organisation of the plastids consists of numerous membrane layers embedded in a material called **stroma.**

Plastids are similar to mitochondria in external structure. Plastids have their own **DNA and ribosomes.**

Vacuoles (Storage):

Vacuoles are storage sacs for solid or liquid contents.

Vacuoles are small-sized in animal cells while plant cells have very large vacuoles [50% to 90% cell volume].

In plant cells, vacuoles are full of cell sap and provide turgidity and rigidity to the cell. In Amoeba, the food'vacuole contain the food items that is consumed it and contractile vacuoles expels excess water and some wastes from the cell.

Comparison between plant & animal cells

Plants cells are different from animal cells structurally. Plant cells have cell walls and chloroplast which are missing in animal cells. Plants cells also have large vacuoles which are either very small or missing in animal cells. The nucleus is present at the centre of the cell in animal cells and at the periphery in plant cells.

Chromatin

Chromatin is a thread-like structure which serves as the genetic material present inside the nucleus of the cell.

It is made up of DNA and protein molecules.

DNA contains the hereditary information needed for the structure and function of the organism.

Cell division:

It is the process of formation of two daughter cells from a single cell following a series of steps.

Mitosis:

It is also known as equational division because it forms exactly a xerox copy of the previous cell.

The DNA amount remains constant and also the chromosome number remains constant in a species.

This is the cell division required for growth and repair of the body as it adds up identical cells to a certain part of the body increasing its size.

In case of injuries where the cells are damaged, mitosis occurs to repair those regions.

Meiosis:

It is known as the reductional division as the chromosome number reduces to half in this type of division.

It can form gametes as gametes need to be haploid cells so that they can fuse together in order to form a diploid zygote which will give rise to a new offspring.

ANIMAL CELL AND PLANT CELL DIAGRAM

Animal Cell Structure
Cell (Plasma) Membrane
Mitochondria
Chromatin
Nucleolus
Peroxisome
Rough Endoplasmic Reticulum
Nucleus
Ribosomes
Vacuole
Smooth Endoplasmic Reticulum
Centrosome
Golgi Apparatus
Microtubules
Golgi Vesicle
Lysosome
Cytoplasm

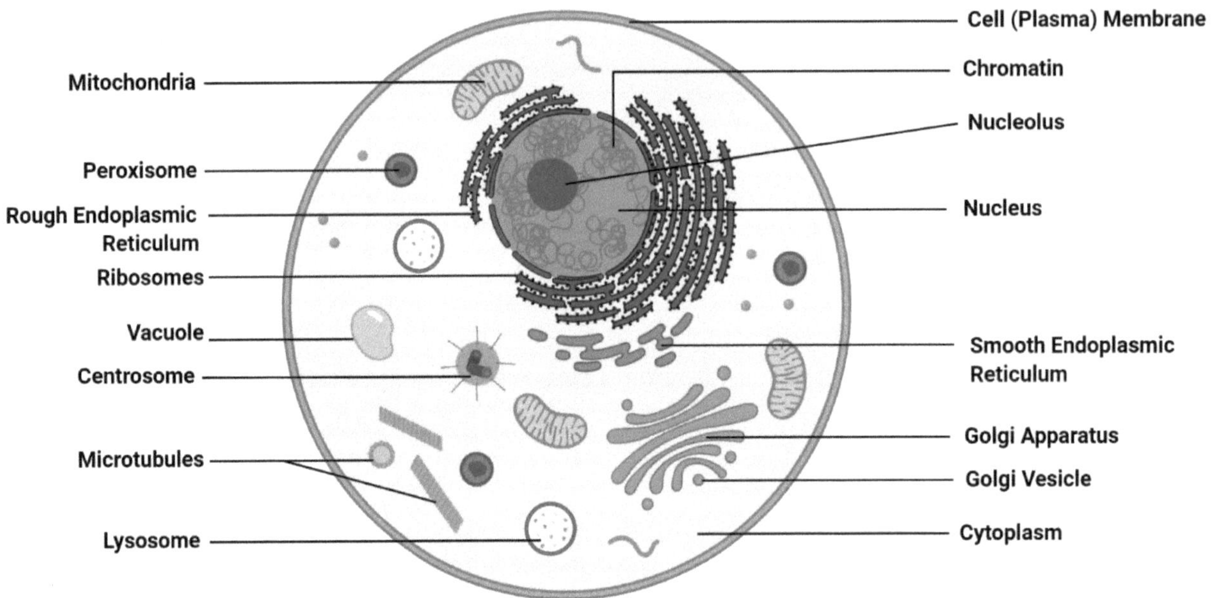

ANIMAL CELL

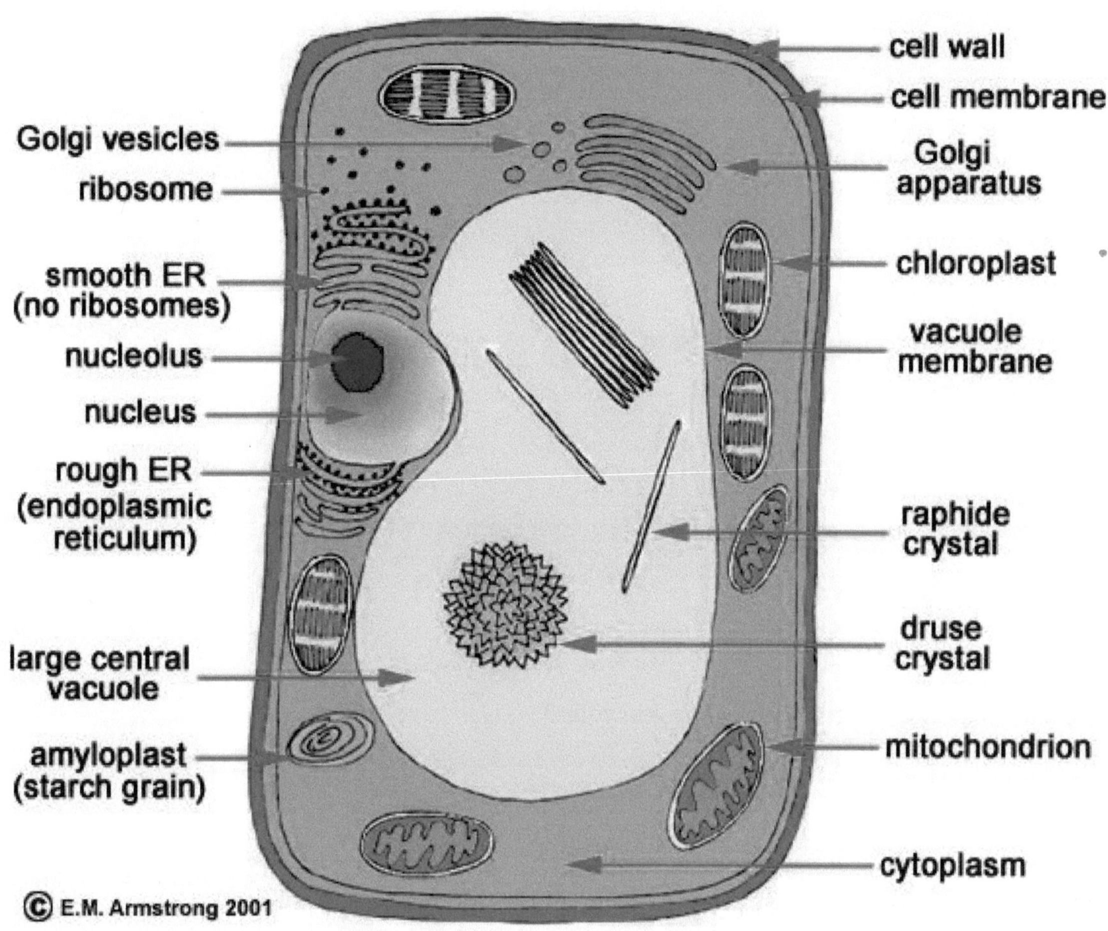

PLANT CELL

IMPORTANT QUESTION

Q1. Explain the types of Plastids in brief.

Q2. Explain the functions and structure of Golgi bodies.

Q3. What is nucleoid?

Q4. What is the difference between plant cells and animal cells?

Q6. What are suicidal bags (lysosomes)?

Q7. What is the function of chromosomes?

Q8. Name the smallest cell in human body?

ANS = The granule cell of the cerebellum is the smallest cell in the body. It measures between 4 and 4.5 micrometers in length

Q9. Which is the largest cell in human body?

Ans = The human egg (ovum) is the largest cell in the body and can be seen without the aid of a microscope. It is one millimeter in diameter.

Q10. Why Plant cells are are more rigid than animal cells?

ANS = Plant cells are more rigid than the animaal cell wass due to the presene of cell wall. Plant cells are made up of an inner and outer cell layer made up of cellulose and lipids.

Q11. Explain the process of osmosis in detail.

Q12. Draw and label diagrams of plant cell and animal cell.

MCQ

1. Colourless plastids are known as

(a) Chromoplasts
(b) Chloroplasts
(c) Leucoplasts
(d) Protoplast

2. Animal cell lacking nuclei would also lack in

(a) Ribosome
(b) Lysosome
(c) Endoplasmic reticulum
(d) Chromosome

3. The phenomenon by which protoplast of a cell shrinks from the wall is

(a) Osmosis
(b) Plasmolysis
(c) Diffusion
(d) Glycolysis

4. Which of the following are examples of prokaryotes?

(a) Algae
(b) Fungi
(c) Bacteria
(d) Protozoa

5. The barrier between the protoplasm and the outer environment in an animal cell is

(a) Cell wall
(b) Plasma membrane
(c) Nuclear membrane
(d) Cytoplasm

6. Ribosomes are the site of

(a) Photosynthesis
(b) Respiration
(c) Protein synthesis
(d) Absorption

7. Which is the largest cell organelle present in plant cell?

(a) Nucleus
(b) Chloroplast
(c) Endoplasmic reticulum
(d) Mitochondria

NCERT SOLUTION

NCERT Textbook for Class 9 Science – Page 59

1. Who discovered cells and how?

Answer- Cell was discovered by an English Botanist, Robert Hooke in 1665. He used self-designed microscope to observe cells in a cork slice back then.

2. Why the cell is called the structural and functional unit of life?

Answer- Cells are called the structural and functional unit of life because all the living organisms are made up of cells and all the functions that take place inside the organisms are performed by cells.

Class 9 Science NCERT Textbook – Page 61

1. How do substances like C02 and water move in and out of the cell? Discuss.

Answer: CO2 moves by diffusion and H2O move by osmosis through cell membrane.

2. Why is the plasma membrane called a selectively permeable membrane?

Answer: It is called selectively permeable membrane because it allows the entry and exit of some substances, not all.

Class 9 Science NCERT Textbook – Page 63

1. Fill in the gaps in the following table illustrating differences between prokaryotic and eukaryotic cells.

Answer:

Prokaryotic Cell	***Eukaryotic***
1. **Size:** Generally small (1–10 μm) (1μm = 10^{-6} m)	1. Size: Generally large (5–100 μm)
2. Nuclear region is poorly defined due to absence of a nuclear membrane and known as nucleoid.	2. Nuclear region well defined and surrounded by a nuclear membrane.
3. There is a single chromosome.	3. There are more than one chromosomes.
4. Membrane-bound cell organelles absent.	4. Membrane-bound cell organelles present.

NCERT Textbook for Class 9 Science – Page 65

1. Can you name the two organelles we have studied that contain their own genetic material?

Answer: The two organelles which have their own genetic material are:

1. Mitochondria 2. Plastids

2. If the organisation of a cell is destroyed due to some physical or chemical influence, what will happen?

Answer: The cell will not be able to revive and lysosomes will digest it.

3. Why are lysosomes known as suicide hags?

Answer: When the cell gets damaged, lysosomes may burst, and the enzymes digest their own cell. Therefore lysosomes are known as suicide bags.

4. Where are proteins synthesised inside the cell?

Answer: The proteins are synthesised in the ribosomes that are also known as protein factories

EXERCISE - PAGE 67

1. Make a comparison and write down ways in which plant cells are also different from animal cells.

Answer:

Plant Cell	***Animal Cell***
1. Plant cells have cell wall. 2. They contain chloroplast. 3. They do not have centriole. 4. Vacuole is large and present in centre of the cell. 5. Nucleus is present in the side of the plant cell.	1. Animal cells don't have a cell wall. 2. They don't have chloroplasts. 3. Centriole is present in them. 4. Vacuole is small. 5. Nucleus is present in the centre of the animal cell.

2. How is a prokaryotic cell different from a eukaryotic cell?

Answer = Prokaryotic cell is generally smaller in size (1-10 PM), nuclear region is poorly defined, the cell organelles are not membrane-bound and has a single chromosome.

Eukaryotic cell is generally larger in size (5-100 PM), nuclear region is well defined with nuclear membrane. Membrane-bound cell organelles are present and has more than one chromosome.

3. What would happen if the plasma membrane ruptures or breaks down?

Answer: If plasma membrane ruptures or breaks down then molecules of some substances will freely move in and out.

4. What would happen to the life of a cell if there was no Golgi apparatus?

Answer- Golgi apparatus performs the function of a storage modification and packaging of products. If Golgi apparatus is not there then materials synthesized by cell will not be packaged and transported.\

5.Which organelle is known as the powerhouse of the cell? Why?

Answer- Mitochondria are known as the powerhouse of cells because energy required for various chemical activities needed to support life is released by mitochondria in the form of ATP (Adenosine triphosphate) molecules.

or

Answer = Mitochondria is known as powerhouse of the cell because it releases the energy required for different activities of life.

6. Where do the lipids and proteins constituting the cell membrane get synthesised?

Answer: Lipids and proteins are synthesised in ER [Endoplasmic Reticulum].

7. How does Amoeba obtain it's food?

Answer: Amoeba take it's food by the cell membrane which forms the food vacuole.

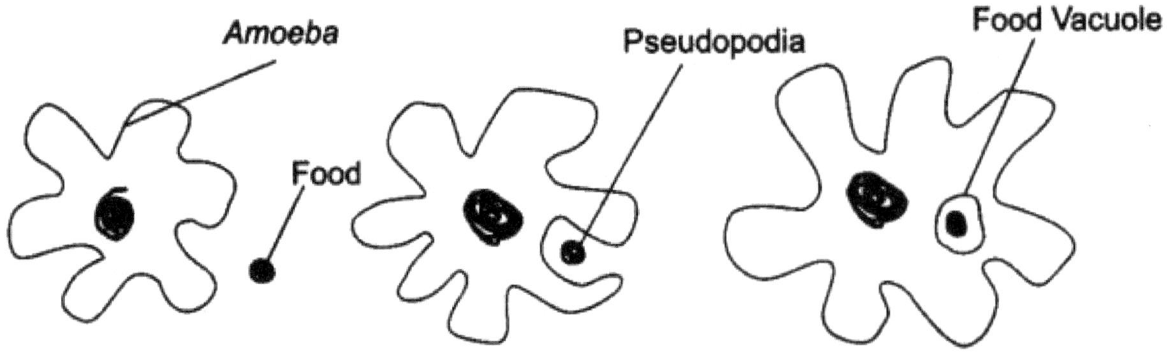

Endocytosis in *Amoeba*

8. What is osmosis?

Answer: Osmosis is the process of movement of water molecule from a region of higher water concentration through a semi-permeable membrane to a region of lower water concentration.

9. Carry out the following osmosis experiment:

Take four peeled potato halves and scoop each one out to make potato cups, one of these potato cups should be made from a boiled potato. Put each potato cup in a trough containing water.

Now,

(a) Keep cup A empty

(b) Put one teaspoon sugar in cup B

(c) Put one teaspoon salt in cup C '

(d) Put one teaspoon sugar in the boiled potato cup D

Keep these for two hours. Then observe the four potato cups and answer the following:

(i) Explain why water gathers in the hollowed portion of B and C.

(ii) Why is potato A necessary for this experiment?

(iii) Explain why water does not gather in the hollowed out portions of A and D.

Answer:

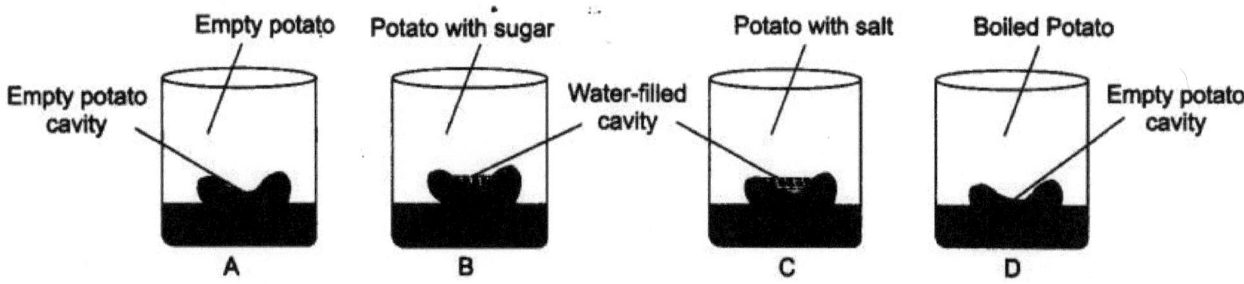

(i) Water gathers in B and C because in both the situations there is difference in the concentration of water in the trough and water in the cup of Potato. Hence, osmosis takes place as the potato cells act as a semi-permeable membrane.

(ii) Potato A is necessary for this experiment for comparison, it acts as a control.

(iii) Water does not gather in the hollowed out portions of A and D. As cup of A does not have change in the concentration for water to flow. For osmosis to occur one of the concentration should be higher than the other.

In cup D, the cells are dead and hence the semi-permeable membrane does not exists for the flow of water and no osmosis takes place

10. Which type of cell division is required for growth and repair of body and which type is involved in formation of gametes?

Answer = Mitosis is the type of cell division that is involved in the growth and repair of the body whereas Meiosis is a type of cell division that results in the formation of gametes.

OR

Whenever new cells are required, mitosis takes place.

It is even the mode of asexual reproduction.

Meiosis on the other hand is the cell division caused in the sexual reproduction.

This is thus involved in the formation of gametes.

SAMPLE PAPER

Maximum time-30 minutes Maximum marks- 25

1. Explain the process of osmosis and give an example. (2 marks)
2. What are the functions of plastids? (3)
3. Explain the difference between Prokaryotic cell and Eukaryotic cell (4 marks)
4. What are genes? What is the difference between genes and chromosomes? (3 marks)
5. Why are lysosomes called suicidal bags? (2 marks)
6. Draw a neat diagram of a plant cell. (4 marks)
7. Write a short note on Plasma Membrane. (3 marks)
8. Why is the inner membrane of Mitochondria folded? (2 marks)
9. Name the smallest and the longest cell in human body. (2 marks)
10. Define nucleoids. (1 mark)

II

TISSUES

NOTES

TISSUES =

Group of cells having a common origin and similar function are termed as tissues.

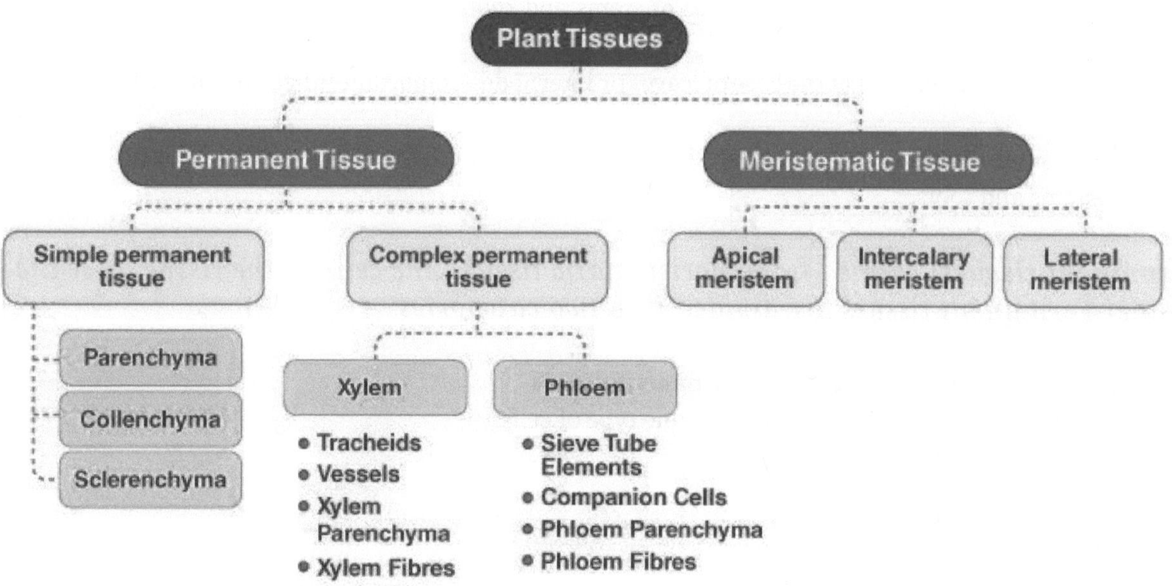

Plant tissues:

On the basis of the dividing capacity, plant tissues are of two types:

1. **Meristematic tissues**
2. **Permanent tissues**

1. Meristematic tissues: *Consist of actively-dividing cells. Meristematic tissues are of three types:*

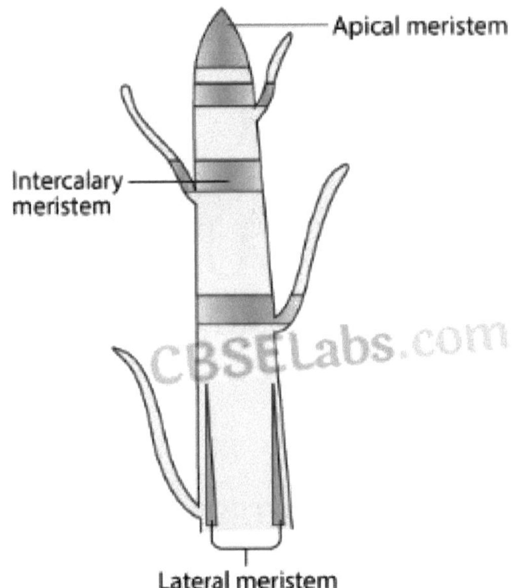

Apical meristem: Present at the growing tips of stems and roots. Important function: To increase the length of stems and roots.

Intercalary meristem: Present at the base of leaves or internodes. Important function: For the longitudinal growth of plants.

Lateral meristem: Present on the lateral sides of the stems and roots. Important function: To increase the thickness of stems and roots.

2. Permanent tissues: *Formed from meristematic tissues, the cells in the tissue loose the ability to divider Permanent tissues are divided into two categories:*

(A) Simple permanent tissues (B) complex permanent tissues

(A) Simple permanent tissue: Consist of only one type of cells.

Types of simple permanent tissues:

Parenchyma:

Composed of unspecialised living cells with relatively thin cell walls, intercellular space, present in soft parts of the plant.

Their main function is storage.

example = chlorenchyma , Aerenchyma

Collenchyma:

Composed of living and elongated cells with cell walls irregularly thickened at the comers. No intercellular space.

It provides mechanical support and elasticity to plant.

It helps in bending of leaves and stems.

Sclerenchyma:

Composed of long, narrow, and thick-walled cells.

This tissue is made up of dead cells and there are no intercellular spaces.

Sclerenchyma cells are dead, present in seeds, nuts, the husk of a coconut, fibres of jute etc

chlorenchyma

Parenchyma cells of leaves containing chlorophyll forms the chlorenchyma .
They carry out the photosynthesis.

Aerenchyma

Parenchyma cells of aquatic plants containing large air cavities forms the aerenchyma.
It gives buoyancy to plants that help them float.

Protective tissue

(a) EPIDERMIS :
Location = outermost layer of all soft parts of the plants like young stems , roots , leaves etc.
Structure = single layer of cell.
In desert plants, covered with waxy coating of **cutin** . Have minute opening **(stomata).**
stomata allows gases exchange and site of transpiration.
Function = Acts as a protective tissue. Allows exchanges of gases yhrough stomata.
(b) CORK :
Location = outermost protective tissue of old stems and roots.
Structure = Made up dead cells.
Function = Impervious to water and gasses due to the presence of **suberin** and prevents entry of microorganisms.
(B) Complex permanent tissue = Made up of more than one type of cells (Conducting tissues).
Xylem: Conducts water and minerals from the roots to the different parts of the plant.
It is a unidirectionals.
Composed of four different types of cells—**tracheids, vessels, xylem parenchyma and xylem fibres.**
Phloem: Conducts food material from the leaves to the different parts of the plant.
It is a Bidirectionals.
Composed of four different types of cells—**sieve tubes, companion cells, phloem parenchyma and phloem fibres.**

XYLEM

It is thicked walled and mostly dead cell.
(i) xylem parenchyma : it is living cells , store food , help in sideway conductionof water.
(ii) xylem fibres : it provide the mechanical support.
(iii) tracheid : Transport water and mineral salts.
(iv) vessels : Transport water and mineral salts.

PHLOEM

It is thin walled and mostly living cell.
(i) phloem parenchyma : stores starch and protein.
(ii) phloem fibres : it provide flexibility and dead cells.
(iii) sieve tubes : cells was contains pores, the end walls are perforated called sieve plates. it transpot sugar and nutrients
(iv) companion cells : help sieve tubes in transport sugar and nutrients.

Animal tissues:

Animal tissues are classified into four types based on the functions they perform:

1. **Epithelial**
2. **Connective**
3. **Muscular**
4. **Nervous**

1. *Epithelial tissues:*

Form the covering of the external surfaces, internal cavities and organs of the animal body. Various types of epithelial tissues are:

(a) Simple squamous epithelium :
Location = Oseophagus and the lining of the mouth .
Structure = A thin flat , single layer of flat cell.
Function = Transport by diffusion and where minimal protection is required.
(b) Stratified squamous epithelium :
Location = Skin
Structure = Arranged in pattern of layer
Function = Prevent wear and tear , protect from mechanical injury.
(c) Cuboidal epithelium
Location = Lining of kidney tubles and ducts of salivary glands.
Structure = cube shaped cells.
function = mechanical support
(d) Columnar epithelium
Location = Inner lining of intestine.
Structure = Tall , pillar like cells.
function = It function is Absorption and scretion .
(e) Ciliated columnar epithelium
Location = Respiratory tract
Structure = hair like projection on outer surface.
function = Movement pushes the mucus.
(f) Glandular epithelium
Location = sweat glands.
Structure = multicellular glands.
Function = secretion.

2. Connective tissues

It is loosely spaced and embedded in an intercellular matrix.
matrix may be jilly like fluid.
(a) Blood
Fluid matrix is composed of plasma.
Function = transports gases , digested food , hormones and waste materials.

EXTRA NOTES FOR BLOOD

BLOOD AND LYMPH

Blood is connective tissues , fluid matrix of blood is plasma having wandering or floating cells, caleed corpuscles , blood helps in the transoortation of various materials such as nutritive substances, gases , excretory products, hormones etc.

PLASMA

It forms 55 % part of blood . it constitute of 90 % - 91 % of water , 7% of protein (Albumin, fibrinogen , globulin) , 0.9% of inorganic salt etc.

CORPUSCLES

Forms 45 % part of blood.

RBCS (Red blood cells)

They are also called as erthyrocytes, containing red coloured respiratory pigment caleed haemolobin that helps in transportation of oxygen.

WBCS (white blood cells)

They are also called as Soldiers of the body.

They are irregular , amoeboid, phagocyte cells that protect our body by engulfing bacterial & other foreign particles.

There are of five types : Monocytes, Lymphocytes, Basophiles , Neutrophiles , Eosinophils.

BLOOD PLATELETS OR THROMBOCYTES

They are spindle shaped cells which are involved in clotting of blood.

Platelets are pieces of very large cells in the bone marrow called **megakaryocytes**

(b) Bone

Hard matrix is composed of calcium and phosphorus compounds.

Function = It forms the framework that supports the body.

(c) Cartilage

Soil matrix is composed of proteins and sugars.

It is soft bone.

Function = Smoothens bones surface at joints.

example = Nose , Ear , trachea , larynx.

(d) Tendon & Ligament

Tendon is fibrous tissue with great strength but limited flexibility.

Tendon connect muscles to bones.

Ligament is very elastic.

Ligament connect bones with bones.

Ligament contain very little matrix.

(e) Areolar Tissue

Present between skin and muscles.

Around blood vessels and nerves.

Fill space inside the organ.

(f) Adipose Tissue

Found below skin and internal organ.

Filled with fat globules.

Acts as an Insulator.

3. Muscular tissues

Muscular tissues consists of elongated cells,also called Muscle fibres.

This tissue is responsible for Movement in our body.

It is a contractile protein.

	Main features	Histology
Skeletal muscle	• Fibers: striated, tubular and multi nucleated • Voluntary • Usually attached to skeleton	
Smooth muscle	• Fibers: non-striated, spindle-shaped, and uninucleated • Involuntary • Usually covering wall of internal organs	
Cardiac muscle	• Fibers: striated, branched and uninucleated • Involuntary • Only covering walls of the heart	

Jack Westin

Type of muscular tissue

(a) Striated muscles or skeletal muscles or voluntary muscles

It is present in Limbs.

it is Striated.

Cells are cylindrical shaped, unbranched , multinucleated.

Function = it is voluntary

(b) Smooth muscles or involuntary muscles

It is present in internal organs.

It is unstriated.

Cells are spindle shaped, unbranched , uninucleated.

Function = It is Involuntary.

(c) Cardiac muscles or involuntary muscles

It is present in heart.

It is striated .

cells are cylindrical shaped , branched , uninucleated .

Function = It is involuntary.

4. Nervous tissue

It is highly specialized.

It is presnt in Brain , Spinal cord , Neurons.

Their functional unit is called Nerve cell or neuron

Nervous tissue is made of neurons that receive and conduct impulses.

Cyton.

Cell body is called cyton which is covered by plasma membrane.

Dendron

Short hair like structure rising from cyton are dendron which are further subdivided into dendrite.

Axon

Axon is long, tail like cylindrical process with fine branches at the end.

Axon is covered by sheath.

Axon of one neuron is very closely packed to the dendrons of anpther neuron to carry impulses from one another neuron in the form of elctrochemical waves.

This close proximity is called as synapse.

IMPORTANT QUESTION

1. Give four differences between bone and cartilage.

2. Give the functions of cartilage.

3. Give difference between xylem and pholem.

4. What is stomata?

5. Why does epidermal tissue have no intercellular space?

6. Name and give the function of each cell of xylem.

7. Why is blood called connective tissue?

8. State the difference between simple tissues of plants.

9. Explain the structure, function and location of nervous tissue.

10. Describe 'epidermis' in plants.

MCQ

1. The cells of cork are dead and have a chemical in their walls that makes them impervious to gases and water. The chemical is

(a) lignin

(b) suberin

(c) cutin

(d) wax

2. The flexibility in plants is due to a tissue called

(a) chlorenchyma

(b) parenchyma
(c) sclerenchyma
(d) collenchyma

3. The tissue present in the lining of kidney tubules and ducts of salivary glands is
(a) squamous epithelium tissue
(b) glandular epithelium tissue
(c) cuboidal epithelium tissue
(d) columar epithelium tissue

4. The connective tissue that connects muscle to bone is called
(a) ligament
(b) tendon
(c) nervous tissue
(d) all of the above

5. The tissue that helps in the movement of our body are
(a) musclar tissue
(b) skeletal tissue
(c) nervous tissue
(d) all of the above

6. Sieve tubes and companion cells are present in
(a) xylem
(b) phloem
(c) cork
(d) cambium

7. The size of the stem increases in the width due to
(a) apical meristem
(b) intercalary meristem
(c) primary meristem
(d) lateral meristem

8. Cartilage and bone are types of
(a) muscular tissue
(b) connective tissue
(c) meristematic tissue
(d) epithelial tissue

9. Xylem and phloem are examples of
(a) epidermal tissue
(b) simple tissue
(c) protective tissue
(d) complex tissue

10. A tissue whose cells are capable of dividing and re-dividing is called
(a) complex tissue
(b) connective tissue
(c) permanent tissue
(d) meristematic tissue

NCERT SOLUTION

NCERT Textbook Page 63

1. What is a tissue?

Ans. A group of cells that are similar in structure and work together to do a peculiar function is called tissue.

2. What is the utility of tissues in multicellular organisms?

Ans. Tissues provide structural strength, mechanical strength, show division of labour.

NCERT Textbook Page 74

1. Name types of simple tissues.

Ans. The types of simple tissues are parenchyma, collenchyma, sclerenchyma and aerenchyma.

2. Where is apical meristem found?

Ans. Apical meristem is found at the tip of root or shoot of the plant.

3. Which tissue makes up the husk of coconut?

Ans. The husk of coconut is made of sclerenchymatous tissue.

4. What are the constituents of phloem?

Ans. Phloem is made up of four types of elements sieve tube, companion cells, phloem fibres and phloem parenchyma.

NCERT Textbook Page 78

1. Name the tisswe responsible for movement in our body.

Ans. 1. Muscular tissue, 2. Nervous tissue, combination of both the tissues are responsible for movement in our body.

2. What does a neuron look like?

Ans. A neuron consists of a cell body with a nucleus and cytoplasm, from which long thin hair like parts arise. Each neuron has a single long part called the axon, and many small, short branched parts called dendrite. An individual nerve cell is called neuron, it may be upto a metre long.\

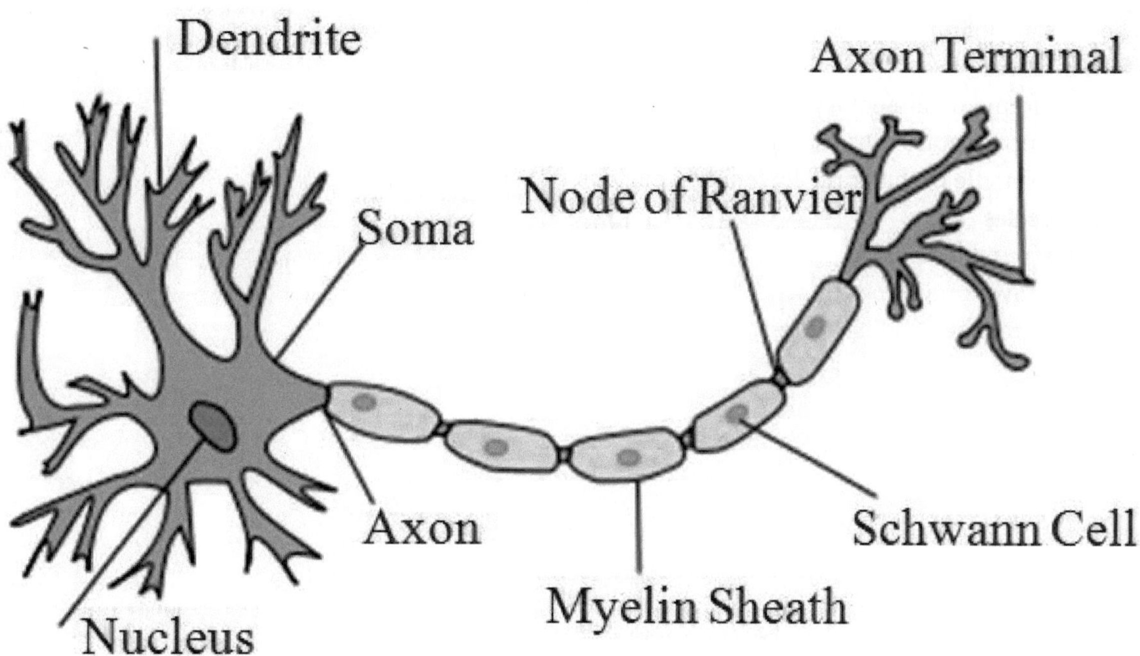

3. Give three features of cardiac muscles.

Answer: Feature of cardiac muscles

(1) Heart muscles (cardiac muscles) are cylindrical, branched and uninucleated

(2) They are striated muscle fibres.

(3) They are involuntary muscles, cannot be controlled by us.

4. What are the Junctions of areolar tissue?

Answer: Areolar tissue are connective tissues found in animal. It is found between skin and muscles, around blood vessels and nerves and in the bone marrow.

It fills the space inside the organs, supports internal organs and helps in the repair of tissues

Questions From NCERT Textbook for Class 9 Science

1. Define the term "tissue".

Answer: Group of cells that are similar in structure and perform same function is called a tissue.

2. How many types of elements together make up the xylem tissue? Name them.

Answer: The xylem is made up of vessels, trachieds, xylem fibres and xylem parenchyma.

3. How are simple tissues different from complex tissues in plants?

Ans. Simple tissues are made up of one type of cells which coordinate to perform a common function. Complex tissues are made up of more than one type of cells. All these coordinate to perform a common function.

4. Differentiate between parenchyma, collenchyma and sclerenchyma on the basis of their cell wall

Ans. Parenchyma: The cells have thin cell walls made up of cellulose.

Collenchyma: The cells have cell walls thickened at the corners due to pectin deposition.

Sclerenchyma: Their walls are thickened due to lignin deposition.

5. What are the functions of stomata?

Ans. The outermost layer of the cell is called epidermis and is very porous. These pores are called stomata. These stomata help in transpiration and exchange of gases.

6. Diagrammaticafty show the difference between the three types of muscle fibres.

Ans. **Striated muscles**

(1) They are connected to bones (Skeletal muscles).

(2) They are voluntary muscles.

(3) The cells are long, cylindrical with many nucleus and are unbranched.

Smooth muscles

(1) They are found in alimentary canal and lungs.

(2) They are involuntary muscles.

(3) They are spindle in shape and have single nucleus.

Cardiac muscles

(1) They are found in heart.

(2) They are involuntary in action.

(3) They are branched and have one nucleus.

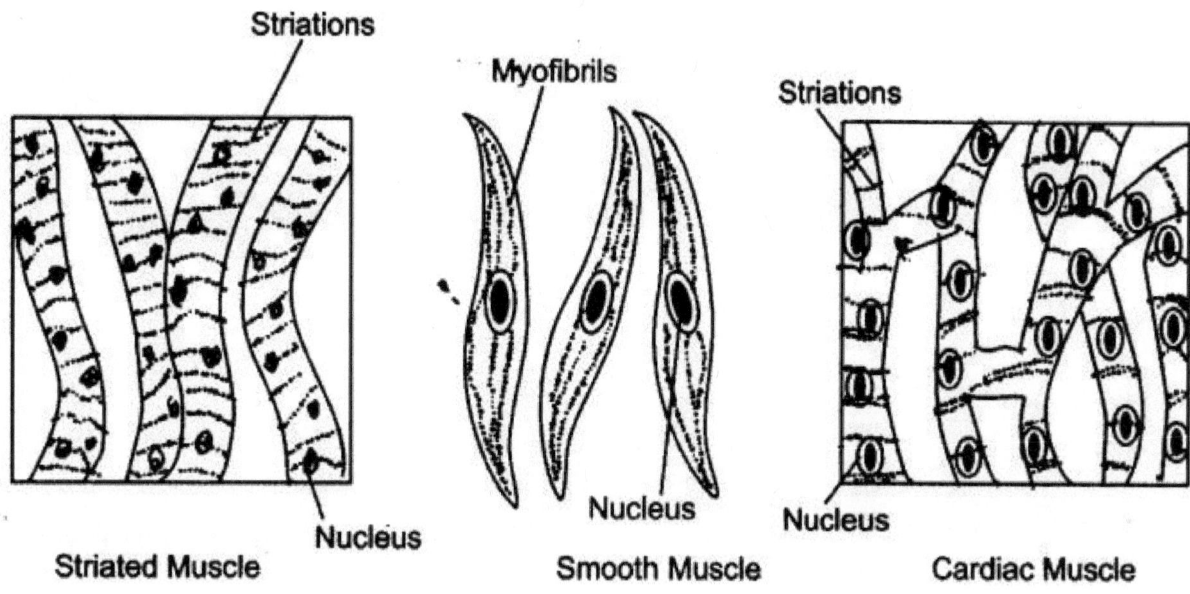

7. What is the specific function of the cardiac muscle?

Ans. (1) Cardiac muscles cells are cylindrical, branched and uninucleated.

(2) They are involuntary muscles.

(3) They show rhythmically contraction and relaxation throughout life.

(4) Their rhythmic contraction and relaxation helps in pumping action of heart.

8. Differentiate between striated, unstiiated and cardiac muscles on the basis of their structure and location in the body.

Answer =

Character	*Striated Muscles*	*Unstriated Muscles*	*Cardiac Muscles*
1. Shape	Cells are long, cylindrical, non-tapering and are unbranched.	Cells are long with tapering ends and are unbranched.	Cells are non-tapering and cylindrical in shape and are branched.
2. Location in body	In hands, legs and skeletal muscles.	The wall of stomach, intestine, ureter and bronchi, etc.	In the heart.
3. Light and dark bands	Present.	Absent.	Present but less prominent.

9. Draw a labelled diagram of neuron.

Answer =

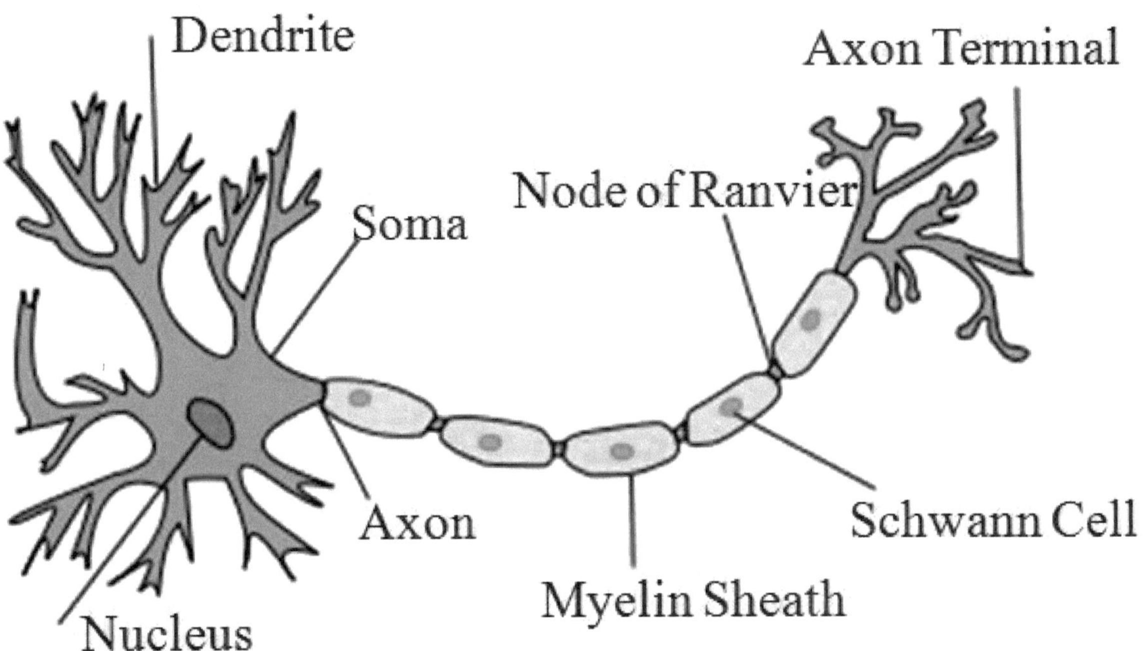

10. Name the following:

(1) Tissue that forms the inner lining of our mouth.

(2) Tissue that connect muscle to bone in humans,

(3) Tissue that transports food in plants.

(4) Tissue that stores fat in our body.

(5) Connective tissue with a fluid matrix:.

(6) Tissue present in the brain.

Answer (1) Squamous epithelium

(2) Tendons

(3) Phloem

(4) Areolar tissue

(5) Blood

(6) Nervous tissue

11. Identify the type of tissue in the following: Skin, bark of tree, bone, lining of kidney tubule, vascular bundle.

Ans. (a) Skin–Striated squamous epithelium

(b) Bark of tree–Cork, protective tissue

(c) Bone–Connective tissue

(d) Lining of kidney tubule–Cuboidal epithelium tisse

(e) Vascular bundle–Conducting tissue

12. Name the regions in which parenchyma tissue is present.

Ans. In the pith of the roots and stems. When it contains chlorophyll, it is called chlorenchyma, found in green leaves. In aquatic plants, parenchyma contains large air cavities and help them to float. Such type of parenchyma is called aerenchyma.

13. What is the role of epidermis in plants?

Ans. Cells of epidermis forms a continuous layer without intercellular spaces. It protects all the parts of plants.

14. How does the cork act as a protective tissue?

Ans. Cork acts as a protective tissue because its cells are dead and compactly arranged without intercellular spaces. They have deposition of suberin on the walls that make them impervious to gases and water.

15. Complete the table:

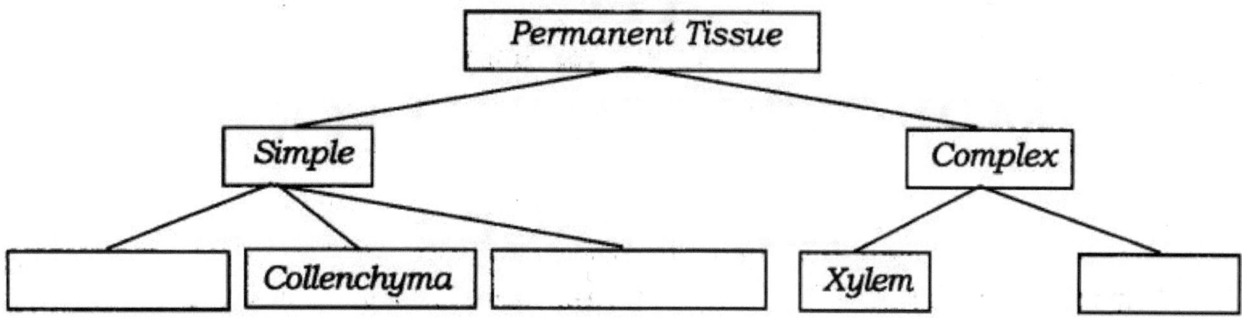

Answer

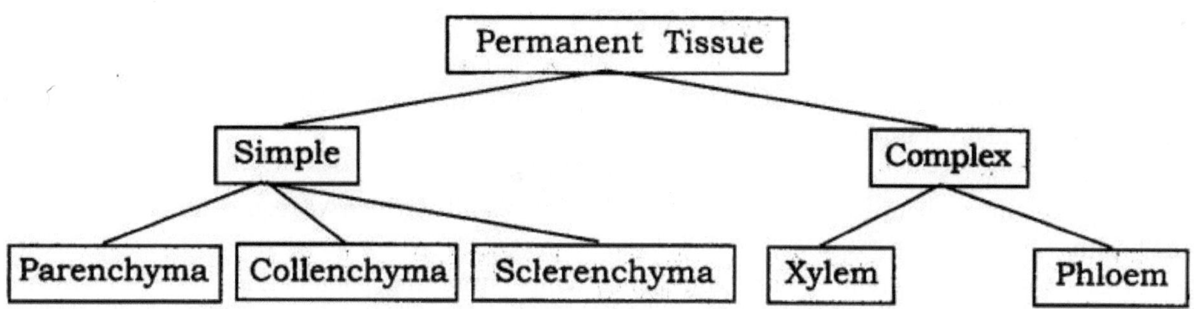

SAMPLE PAPER

Maximum marks- 30 Maximum time- 45 mins

1. Write a note on plant tissues? (5 marks)
2. What is the function of connective tissues? Explain its types. (4 marks)
3. Draw a structure of a nerve cell (neuron). (3 marks)
4. What is the region where parenchyma tissue is present? (2 marks)
5. What is the point of difference between cardiac muscle and striated muscle? (2 marks)
6. Draw a neat diagram of a smooth muscle. (3marks)
7. Where is epical tissue present? (1 mark)
8. What are the various types of an animal tissue? (5 marks)
9. Write the difference between xylem and phloem. (3 marks)
10. Write the difference between a bone and cartilage. (2 marks)

III

IMPROVEMENT IN FOOD RESOURCES

NOTES

Plant and animal breeding and selection for quality improvement and management, Use of fertilizers, Manures, Protection from pests and diseases, Organic farming.

Facts that Matter

• Food supplies proteins, carbohydrates, fats, vitamins and minerals, all of which we require for body development, growth and health.

• Different crops require different climatic conditions, temperature and photoperiods for their growth and completion of their life cycle. Photoperiods are related to the duration of sunlight. Growth of plants and flowers are dependent on sunlight.

• **Successful crop production depends upon many factors such as:**

(i) Understanding how crops grow and develop.

(ii) Effect of various nutrients, climate, water on the growth of the plant.

(iii) Modification and management of each factor for increasing the yield of the crop.

• The crops which are grown in rainy season (the kharif season, from June to October) are called as **kharif crops.**

Example: Paddy, soyabean, pigeon pea, maize, cotton, green gram and black gram are kharif crops.

• The crops which are grown in winter season (the rabi season, from November to April) are called **rabi crops.**

Example: Wheat grain, peas, mustard and linseed are rabi crops.

• **Crop variety improvement:** It can be done either by hybridisation or by introducing a gene.

(i) Crop improvement by hybridisation: Hybridisation refers to crossing between genetically dissimilar plants. This crossing may be intervarietal (between different varieties), interspecific (between two different species of the same genus) or intergeneric (between different genera).

(ii) Crop improvement by introducing a gene: This provides the desired characteristics and results in genetically modified crops.

• Cultivation practices and crop yield are related to weather, soil quality and availability of water. Since weather conditions such as drought and flood situations are unpredictable, varieties that can be grown in diverse climatic conditions are useful.

• **The factors for which variety improvement is done are:**

(i) Higher yield: To increase productivity of the crop per acre.

(ii) Improved quality: The quality of crop products vary from crop to crop. E.g., protein quality is important in pulses, oil quality in oilseeds, preserving quality in fruits and vegetables.

(iii) Biotic and abiotic resistance: Biotic factors are the diseases, insects and nematodes while abiotic factors are the drought, salinity, water logging, heat, cold and frost which affect the crop productivity. Varieties resistant to these factors (stresses) can be improved to increase crop production.

(iv) Change in maturity duration: Shorter maturity period of crop reduces the cost of crop production and makes the variety economical. Uniform maturity makes the harvesting process easy and reduces losses during harvesting.

(v) Wider adaptability: It allows the crops to be grown under different climatic conditions in different areas.

(vi) Desirable agronomic characteristics: It increases productivity, for example, tallness and profuse branching are desirable characters for fodder crops; while dwarfness is desired in cereals, so that less nutrients are consumed by these crops.

• **Plant nutrients:** Nutrients are supplied to plants by air, water and soil. There are sixteen nutrients which are essential for plants. Air supplies carbon and oxygen; hydrogen comes from water and soil supplies the other thirteen nutrients to plants. Amongst these thirteen nutrients, six are required in large quantities and are therefore called macro-nutrients. The other seven nutrients are used by plants in small quantities and are therefore called **micro-nutrients.**

• **Nutrients supplied by air, water and soil**

Source	Nutrients
Air	Carbon, Oxygen
Water	Hydrogen, Oxygen
Soil	(*i*) **Macro-nutrients:** Nitrogen, phosphorus, potassium, calcium and sulphur. (*ii*) **Micro-nutrients:** Iron, manganese, boron, zinc, copper, molybdenum and chlorine.

Manure: Manure contains large quantities of organic matter and also supplies small quantities of nutrients to the soil. Manure is prepared by the decomposition of animal excreta and plant waste. Manure helps in enriching soil with nutrients and organic matter and increasing soil fertility. On the basis of the kind of biological waste used to make manure,

It can be classified into three types: (i) Compost (ii) Vermi-compost (iii) Green manure.

(i) Compost: It can be farm waste material such as livestock excreta (cow dung etc.), vegetables waste, animal refuse, domestic waste, sewage waste, straw, eradicated weeds, etc. This material is decomposed in pits and this process of decomposition is also called composting. This compost is rich in organic matter and nutrients.

(ii) Vermi-compost: The compost which is made by the decomposition of plant and animal refuse with the help of redworm is called vermi-compost.

(iii) Green manure: Prior to the sowing of the crop seeds, some plants like sun hemp or guar are grown and then mulched by ploughing them into the soil. These green plants thus turn into green manure which helps in enriching the soil in nitrogen and phosphorus.

• **Fertilizers:** Fertilizers are commercially produced plant nutrients. Fertilizers supply nitrogen, phosphorus and potassium. They are used to ensure good vegetative growth (leaves, branches and flowers), giving rise to healthy plants. Fertilizers are an important factor in the higher yields of high-cost farming.

• **Organic farming:** It is a farming system with minimal or no use of chemicals as fertilizers, herbicides, pesticides, etc. and with a maximum input of organic manures, recycled farm-wastes (straw and livestock excreta), use of bio-agents such as culture of blue-green algae in preparation of biofertilizers, neem leaves or turmeric specifically in grain storage as bio-pesticides with healthy cropping systems [mixed cropping inter-cropping and crop rotation].

These cropping systems are beneficial in insect, pest and weed control besides providing nutrients.

• **Irrigation:** Proper irrigation is very important for the success of crops. Ensuring that the crop gets water at the right stages during their growing season, can increase the expected yield of a crop. Different kinds of irrigation systems include wells, canals, rivers and tanks.

(i) Wells: These are of two types namely dug wells and tube wells. In a dug well, water is collected from water bearing strata. Tube wells can tap water from the deeper strata. From these wells, water is lifted by pumps for irrigation.

(ii) River lift system: In areas where canal flow is insufficient or irregular due to inadequate reservoir release, the lift system is more rational. Water is directly drawn from the rivers for supplementing irrigation in areas close to rivers.

(iii) Tanks: These are small storage reservoirs, which intercept and store the run-off of smaller catchment areas.

• **Cropping patterns:** It includes different ways of growing crops so as to get the maximum benefit. These different ways include the following:

(i) Mixed cropping: Mixed cropping is growing two or more crops simultaneously on the same piece of land, for example, wheat + gram, or wheat + mustard, or groundnut + sunflower. This reduces disease risk and gives some insurance against failure of one of the crops.

(ii) Inter-cropping: It involves growing two or more crops simultaneously on the same field in definite proportion or pattern. A few rows of one crop alternate with a few rows of a second crop, for example, soyabean + maize, or finger millet (bajra) + cowpea (lobia). The crops are selected such that their nutrient requirements are different. This ensures maximum utilisation of the nutrients supplied, and also prevents pests and diseases from spreading to all the plants belonging to one crop in a field. This way, both crops can give better returns.

(ii) Crop rotation: The growing of different crops on a piece of land in a preplanned succession is known as crop rotation. Depending upon the duration, crop rotation is done for different crop combinations. The availability of moisture and irrigation facilities decide the choice of the crop to be cultivated after one harvest. If crop rotation is done properly then two or three crops can be grown in a year with good harvest.

• **The food requirements of dairy animals are of two types:**

(a) maintenance requirement which is the food required to support the animals to live a healthy life, and (b) milk producing requirement, which is the type of food required during the lactation period.

• **Weeds:** Weeds are unwanted plants in the cultivated field, for example, Xanthium (gokhroo), Parthenium (gazar ghas) and Cyperinus rotundus (motha). They compete for food, space and light. Weeds take up nutrients and reduce the growth of the crop. Therefore, removal of weeds from cultivated fields during the early stages of crop growth is essential for a good harvest.

• **Methods of weed control:** The most effective method is the mechanical removal. Preventive methods such as proper seed bed preparation, finely sowing of crops, inter-cropping and croprotation also help in weed control.

• **Insect pests:** Generally insect pests attack the plants in three ways: (i) They cut the root, stem and leaf, (ii) they suck the cell sap from various parts of the plant, and (iii) They bore into stem and fruits. They thus affect the health of the crop and reduce yields.

• **Preventive measures against pest include:**

(i) The use of disease resistant varieties.

(ii) Growing two or more crops simultaneously on the same field.

(iii) Summer ploughing: In this method, fields are ploughed deep in summers to destroy both pests as well as weeds.

• Animal husbandry is the scientific management of animal livestock. It includes various aspects such as feeding, breeding and disease control. Animal-based farming includes cattle, goat, sheep, poultry and fish farming.

• Milk producing females are called milch animals (dairy animals), while the one used for farm labour are called draught animals.

• **Animal feed includes:** (a) Roughage, which is largely, fibre and (b) Concentration which are low in fibre and contain relatively high levels of protein and other nutrients.

• **The improved poultry breeds are developed for the following desirable traits:**

(i) Number and quality of chicks.

(ii) Dwarf broiler parent for commercial chick production.

(iii) Summer adaptation capacity.

(iv) Low maintenance requirements.

(v) Reduction in the size of the egg-laying bird with ability to utilise more fibrous cheaper diets formulated using agricultural by-products.

• **Production of poultry birds:** For good production of poultry birds, good management practices are important. These include maintenance of temperature and hygenic conditions in housing and poultry feed, as well as prevention and control of diseases and pests.

The housing, nutritional and environmental requirements of broilers are somewhere different from those of egg layers. The ration (daily food requirement) for broilers is protein rich with adequate fat. The level of vitamins A and K is kept high in the poultry feeds.

• **Fish Production:** There are two ways of obtaining fish. One is from natural resources, which is called capture fishing. The other way is by fish farming, which is called culture fishery.

• **Popular marine fish varieties include**: Pomphret, mackerel, tuna, sardines and Bombay duck. Marine fish of high economic value includes mullets, bhetki pearl spots, prawns, mussels and oysters.

• As marine fish stocks get further depleted, the demand for more fish can only be met by culture fisheries, a practice called mariculture.

• **Fish resources are of two types:**

(a) Fresh water resources such as canals, ponds, reservoirs and rivers.

(b) Brackish water resources (where sea water and fresh water mix together) such as estuaries and lagoons.

• More extensive fish farming can be done in composite fish culture systems. Both local and imported fish species are used in such systems.

In such a system, a combination of five or six species is used in a single fish pond. These species are selected so that they do not compete for food among them having different types of food habits. As a result, the food available in all parts of the pond is used.

IMPORTANT QUESTION

1. Do organisms need food?

2. What does food provide?

3. Do you know what are the major sources of food?

4. Name the organism used in the preparation of vermicompost.

5. Name two fertilisers supplying N, P, K to crops.

6. What are the factors on which irrigation requirements depend?

7. What are the various irrigation systems adopted in India?

8. Give any two differences between micro and macro nutrients.

9. What is hybridisation in plants? Mention any two desired characters for which it is done.

10. How does the use of fertilisers improve crop production?

11. Though fertilisers increase crop production, they are to be used in limited amount. Why?

MCQ

1. Using fertilizers in farming is an example of

I. No cost production

II. Low cost production

III. High cost production

IV. None of these

2. Nitrogen, phosphorus and potassium are examples of

I. Micro-nutrients

II. Macro-nutrients

III. Fertilizers

IV. Both I and II

3. Cyperinus and Parthenium are types of

I. Diseases

II. Pesticides

III. Weeds

IV. Pathogens

4. Mullets, prawns, mussels are examples of

I. Marine fishes

II. Fresh-water fishes

III. Finned fishes

IV. Shell fish

5. What is the other name for Apis cerana indica?

I. Indian cow

II. Indian buffalo

III. Indian bee

IV. None of these

6. The management and production of fish is called

I. Pisciculture

II. Apiculture

III. Sericulture

IV. Aquaculture

7. Rohu and catla are types of

I. Freshwater fish

II. Marine water fish

III. Both I and II

IV. None of these

8. Pasturage is related to

I. Cattle

II. Fishery

III. Apiculture

IV. Sericulture

9. What is the process of growing two or more crops in a definite pattern?

I. Crop rotation

II. Inter-cropping

III. Mixed cropping

IV. Organic cropping

10. Leghorn is related to

I. Apiculture

II. Dairy farming

III. Pisciculture

IV. Poultry

NCERT SOLUTION

NCERT Textbook Page 204

1. What do we get from cereals, pulses, fruits and vegetables?

Ans. Cereals give carbohydrates which provide energy.

Pulses give proteins which build our body.

Vegetables and fruits provide vitamins and minerals.

NCERT Textbook Page 205

1. How do biotic and abiotic factors affect crop production?

Ans. Factors responsible for loss of grains, during storage and production are:

(a) Biotic factors like rodents, pests, insects, etc.

(b) Abiotic factors like temperature, humidity, moisture, etc. Combination of both biotic and abiotic factors causes :

(i) infestation of insects

(ii) weight loss

(iii) poor germination ability

(iv) degradation in quality

(v) discolouration

(vi) poor market price

2. What are the desirable agronomic characteristics for crop improvements?

Ans. Desirable agronomic characteristics for crop improvements are:

(a) Tallness and profuse branching are desirable characters for fodder crops.

(b) Dwarfness is desired in cereals, so that less nutrients are consumed by these crops.

NCERT Textbook Page 205

1. What are macro-nutrients and why are they catted macro-nutrients?

Ans. Macro-nutrients are the essential elements which are utilised by plants in large quantities. Many macro-nutrients are required by the plants for the following functions:

- As the constituent of protoplasm
- N, P, S are present in proteins
- Ca is present in cell wall
- Mg is important constituent of chlorophyll

2. How do plants get nutrients?

Ans. Plants get nutrients from air, water and soil. There are sixteen nutrients essential for the growth of plants. Carbon and Oxygen are supplied by water. The remaining thirteen nutrients are supplied by soil.

NCERT Textbook Page 207

1. Compare the use of manure and fertilizers in maintaining soil fertility.

Ans. Effects of using manures on soil quality:

(i) The manures enrich the soil with nutrients.

(ii) They provide a lot of organic matter (humus) to the soil and thus restores water retention capacity of sandy soils and drainage in clayey soil.

(iii) The addition of manures reduces soil erosion.

(iv) They provide food for soil organisms, like soil friendly bacteria.

Effects of using fertilizers on soil quality:

(i) By the continuous use of fertilizers, the soil becomes powdery, dry and rate of soil erosion increases.

(ii) By the use of fertilizers, the organic matter decreases which further decreases the porosity of soil and the plant roots do not get oxygen properly.

(iii) The nature of soil changes to acidic or basic.

NCERT Textbook Page 208

1. Which of the following conditions will give the most benefits? Why?

(a) Farmers use high-quality seeds, do not adopt irrigation or use fertilizer.

(b) Farmers use ordinary seeds, adopt irrigation and use fertilizer.

(c) Farmers use quality seeds, adopt irrigation, use fertilizer and use crop protection measures.

Ans. In this, (c) Farmers use quality seeds, adopt irrigation, use fertilizer and use crop protection measures.

Use of any quality seeds is not sufficient until they are properly irrigated, enriched with fertilizers and protected from biotic factors. Hence, option (c) will give the most benefits.

NCERT Textbook Page 208

1. Why should preventive measures and biological control methods be preferred for protecting crops?

Ans. Diseases in plants are caused by pathogens. To get rid of pathogens, some preventive measures and biological control methods are used as they are simple, economic and minimise pollution without affecting the soil quality.

2. What factors may be responsible for losses of grains during storage?

Ans. The factors responsible for losses of grains during storage are:

(i) Abiotic factors like moisture (present in food grains), humidity (of air) and temperature.

(ii) Biotic factors like insects, rodents, birds, mites, bacteria and fungi.

NCERT Textbook Page 210

1. Which method is commonly used for improving cattle breeds and why?

Ans. Cross breeding is a process in which indigenous varities of cattle are crossed by exotic breeds to get a breed which is high yielding. During cross breeding, the desired characters are taken into consideration. The offspring should be high yielding, should have early maturity and should be resistant to climatic conditions.

NCERT Textbook Page 211

1. Discuss the implications of the following statement:

"It is interesting to note that poultry is India�s most efficient converter of low fibre food stuff (which is unfit for human consumption) into highly nutritious animal protein food".

Ans. The basic aim of poultry farming is to raise domestic fowl for egg production and chicken meat. These poultry birds are not only the efficient converters of agricultural by-products, particularly cheaper fibrous wastes (which is unfit for human consumption but can be formulated into cheaper diets for poultry birds) into high quality meat and also help in providing egg, feathers and nutrient rich manure. For this reasons, it is said that, "poultry is India's most efficient converter of low fibre food stuff into highly nutritious animal protein food".

NCERT Textbook Page 211

1. What management practices are common in dairy and poultry farming?

Ans. **1. Shelter**: Dairy animals and poultry birds require proper shelter, i.e., well designed dairy and hygienic shelter.

2. Feeding: To get good yield of food product, proper feed is provided to dairy animals and poultry birds.

3. Caring for animal health: Animal and birds must be protected from diseases caused by virus, bacteria or fungi.

2. What are the differences between broilers and layers and in their management?

Ans. The poultry bird groomed for obtaining meat is called broiler. The egg laying poultry bird is called layer.

The housing, nutritional and environmental requirements of broilers are somewhat different from those of egg layers.

The ration (daily food requirement) for broilers is protein rich with adequate fat. The level of vitamins A and K is kept high in the poultry feeds while layers require enough space and proper lightning.

NCERT Textbook Page 213

1. How are fish obtained?

Ans. There are two ways of obtaining fish. One is from natural resources, which is called capture fishing. The other way is by fish farming, which is called culture fishery.

2. What are the advantages of composite fish culture?

Ans. In composite fish culture, a combination of five or six fish species is used in a single fish pond.

These species are selected so that they do not compete for food among them and are having different types of food habits. As a result, the food available in all the parts of the pond is used. For example, Catlas are surface feeders, Rohus feed in the middle-zone of the pond, Mrigals and Common Carps are bottom feeders and Grass Carps feed on the weeds, together these species can use all the food in the pond without competing with each other. This increases the fish yield from pond.

NCERT Textbook Page 213

1. What are the desirable characters of bee varieties suitables suitable for honey production?

Ans. (i) The variety of bee should be able to collect a large amount of honey.

(ii) The bees should stay in a given beehive for a longer period.

(iii) The bees should have capacity of breeding well.

(iv) The variety of bee should be disease resistant.

2. What is pasturage and how is it related to honey production?

Ans. The pasturage means the flowers available to the bees for nectar and pollen collection. In addition to adequate quantities of pasturage, the kind of flowers available will determine the taste of the honey.

Questions From NCERT Textbook

1. Explain any one method of crop production which ensures high yield.

Ans. One method used for crop production which ensures high yield is plant breeding. It is the science involved in improving the varieties of crops by breeding plants. The plants from different areas/places is picked up with desired traits and then hybridisation or cross-breeding of these varieties is done to obtain a plant/ crop of desired characteristic.

The high yielding crop variety shows the following characteristics: High yield, early maturation, less water for irrigation, better quality seeds are produced, less fertilizers required, adapts itself to the environmental conditions.

2. Why are manure and fertilizers used infields?

Ans. They are used to ensure good vegetative growth (leaves, branches and flowers), giving rise to healthy plants, that results in high crop production.

3. What are the advantages of inter-cropping and crop rotation?

Ans. **Advantages of using inter-cropping:**

(i) It helps to maintain soil fertility.

(ii) It increases productivity per unit area.

(iii) Save labour and time.

(iv) Both crops can be easily harvested and processed separately.

Advantages of using crop rotation:

(i) It improves the soil fertility.

(ii) It avoids depletion of a particular nutrient from soil.

(iii) It minimise pest infestation and diseases. (iv) It helps in weed control.

(v) It prevents change in the chemical nature of the soil.

4. What is genetic manipulation? How is it useful in agricultural practices?

Ans. Genetic manipulation is a process of incorporating desirable (genes) characters into crop varieties by hybridisation. Hybridisation involves crossing between genetically dissimilar plants. This is done for production of varieties with desirable characteristics like profuse branching in fodder crops, high yielding varieties in maize, wheat, etc. Genetic manipulation is useful in developing varieties which shows:

- Increased yield
- Better quality
- Shorter and early maturity period
- Better adaptability to adverse environmental conditions
- Desirable characteristics

5. How do storage grain losses occur?

Ans. The factors responsible for loss of grains during storage are:

(i) Abiotic factors like moisture (present in foodgrains), humidity (of air) and temperature.

(ii) Biotic factors like insects, rodents, birds, mites and bacteria.

6. How do good animal husbandry practices benefit farmers?

Ans. Good animal husbandry practices are beneficial to the farmers in the following ways:

(i) Improvement of breeds of the domesticated animals.

(ii) Increasing the yield of foodstuffs such as milk, eggs and meat.

(iii) Proper management of domestic animals in terms of shelter, feeding, care and protection against diseases.

Which ultimately helps the farmers to improve their economic condition.

7. What are the benefits of cattle farming?

Ans. Cattle farming is beneficial in the following ways:

(i) Milk production is increased by high yielding animals.

(ii) Good quality of meat, fibre and skin can be obtained.

(iii) Good breed of draught animals can be obtained.

8. For increasing production, what is common in poultry, fisheries and bee-keeping?

Ans. Through cross breeding, the production of poultry, fisheries and bee-keeping can be increased.

9. How do you differentiate between capture fishing, mariculture, and aquaculture?

Ans. **Capture fishing:** It is the fishing in which fishes are captured from natural resources like pond, sea water and estuaries.

Mariculture: It is the culture of fish in marine water. Varieties like prawns oysters, bhetki and mullets are cultured for fishing.

Aquaculture: It is done both in fresh water and in marine water.

SAMPLE PAPER

Maximum time- 35 minutes Maximum marks- 25

1. Name few common practices used for dairy industry. (4 marks)

2. Explain different types of fisheries. (5 marks)

3. Give any two differences between manure and fertilizers. (2 marks)

4. What are the different cropping systems? (3 marks)

5. How can weeds be controlled? (3 marks)

6. What is the difference between egg-layers and boilers? (2 marks)

7. What are manures? How are they classified? (4 marks)

8. Name any two Indian cattle. (2marks)

Printed by Libri Plureos GmbH in Hamburg,
Germany